T0065558

TICKLING THE IVORIES

PIANO LESSON ANECDOTES

JOHN MATTESON

authorHOUSE®

AuthorHouse™
1663 Liberty Drive
Bloomington, IN 47403
www.authorhouse.com
Phone: 1 (800) 839-8640

Published by AuthorHouse   04/22/2017

ISBN: 978-1-5049-6563-7 (sc)
ISBN: 978-1-5049-6558-3 (e)

Library of Congress Control Number: 2015920258

Print information available on the last page.

This book is printed on acid-free paper.

Acknowledgments

I wish to give special thanks to the following people for helping me make this project become a reality:

My mother Janice White, my aunt Doris Peterson, my grandmother Velma Peterson, my daughter Samantha Matteson, my brothers Mark Matteson {Big Mark}, Mark Fortier {Little Mark} and Brad Fortier, my friend and bassist Geoff Neuman, Amanda Lovecchio, a constant flow of inspiration from Alice Tchekidjian, the one and only Jimmy Antonelli {Flem} and all my amazing and talented piano students.

Introduction

After nearly 30 years as a piano teacher of hundreds of students, mostly children, I find that I continue to be impressed by their musical talent and amused by their unexpected comments. If you like kids as much as I do you will appreciate some of their unintentional and frequently uninhibited humor. Quoting my late Grandmother Velma Peterson, as she quoted a favorite TV host, "Kids say the damnedest things".

I hope you enjoy the following anecdotes that range from the innocent comments of 6 year olds to the sarcastic rejoinders of teenagers. Perhaps when you share them with friends, and especially piano players, they will LOL.

Six Year Olds

During Emily's lesson she got frustrated and yelled, "Why do I have to play the piano? I didn't sign up for this."

After Christina played the first line of her piece with a lot of mistakes I said, "Oh, Christina, lets go back to the beginning and try that again." She turned to me and asked. "What! You didn't get any of that?"

When Christina was to be introduced to eighth notes I began by reviewing the names of the notes she had already learned. She was able to identify the whole note, half note and quarter note and as soon as I pointed to a newly pair of eighth notes and asked what she thought they might be she excitedly blurted out "head phones!"

♫

After Christina stumbled through a song that she neglected to practice I insisted that she try it again. Disgruntled she folded her arms and asked "how much am I getting paid for this?"

After Katherine had gotten all her Ear Training Exercises with sharps correct I told her she did a great job. She proudly said, "I'm pretty sharp with sharps."

When introducing Myles to the dotted half note I placed my finger over the dot and asked, "What's that?" He replied, "A half note." When I pulled my finger away to expose the dot I said, "Now we have a ..." Myles interrupted and blurted out with great enthusiasm, "Half note - period!"

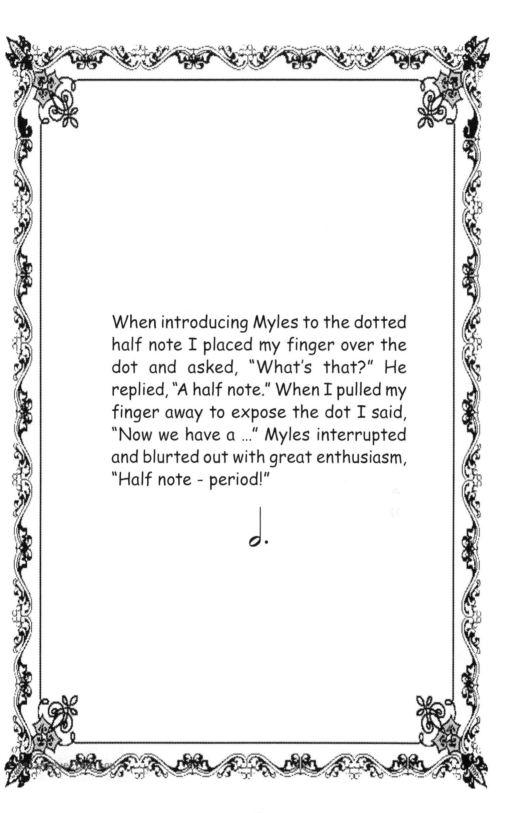

At the beginning of Christina's lesson I sat at the piano and started playing a pretty song that I thought she might like. About half-way through the piece she interrupted, "I'm going to go play in my room. Come get me when you're done."

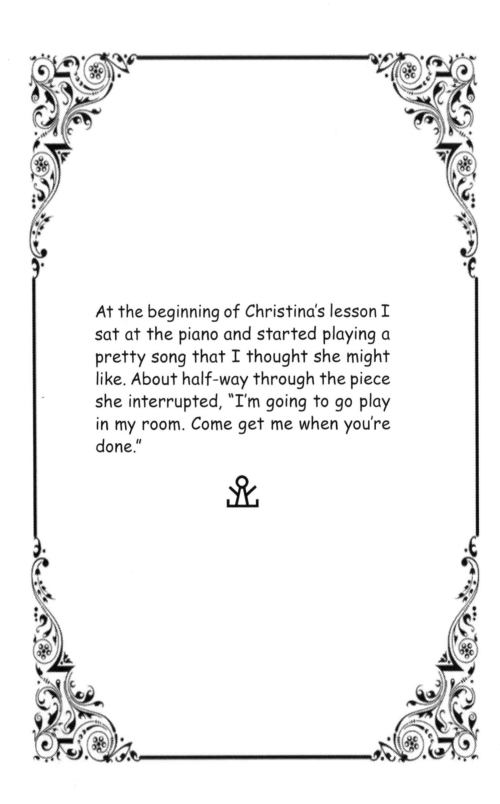

Alex was having trouble recognizing bass clef notes. I told her that I was going to bring flash cards to her next lesson so we could drill them. She said, "Drill? Is that gonna hurt?"

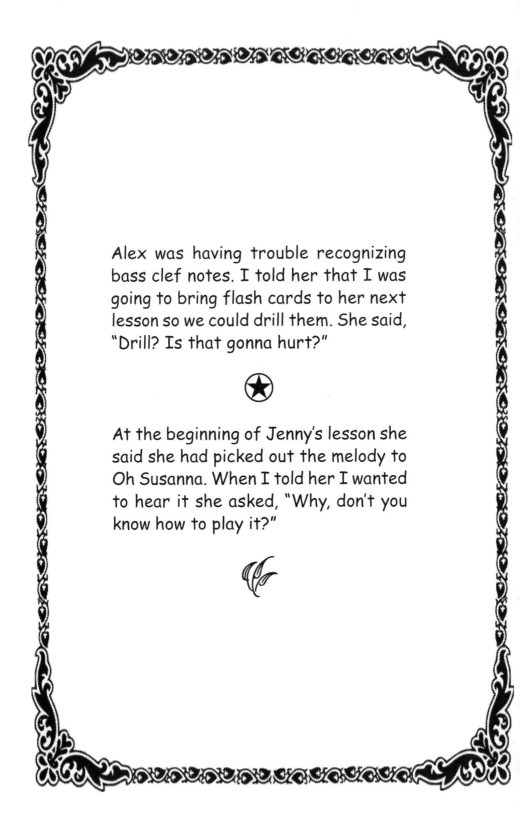

At the beginning of Jenny's lesson she said she had picked out the melody to Oh Susanna. When I told her I wanted to hear it she asked, "Why, don't you know how to play it?"

Assigning Sasha a new piece I told her it was going to be easy to learn because I knew she would be familiar with the melody. When I put Jolly 'ol Saint Nicholas in front of her she remarked, "I don't know this song." Puzzled by this I looked at her mother who said, "We're Jewish."

Seven Year Olds

Seven year old Zoe heard her six year old sister Chloe admit that she hadn't practiced. Giggling Zoe asked
"Is Chloe going to get fired from piano?"

When I arrived at Emmy's house for her lesson I was dressed comfortably in shorts, tee shirt and sandals.
Upon opening the door Emmy looked me up and down and said, " you look homeless."

Nine year old Mike and his seven year old brother took back to back lessons. At the end of Jake's lesson I said, "We still have five minutes left Jake, should we donate them to your brother?" He quickly replied, "Yeah, he needs it."

I asked Akemi at her first lesson if she already knew anything about the piano. She placed her fingers on the black keys and said, "These are the Oriental notes."

Myles came to the end of a song he had been practicing all week, looked at me and said, "I cried so much when I practiced this song that I got a headache."

Upon arriving at the Smith's to give their two daughters their lessons I was asked by seven year old Madelaine if she could be first. I said, "Oh sure, I'm easy 'cause I'm the Man." She looked at me and said, "Excuse me, but my Dad's the Man."

Myles was being introduced to the primary chords and the roman numerals that identify them. I reminded him that the I chord is called a Triad. When I pointed to the root position four note V7 chord he yelled out excitedly, "A Quadrad."

Amanda told her Mom she wanted to quit piano lessons. When Mom said "No" Amanda continued, "But Mom they're so expensive. Just think how much money you'll save. If you need me to quit, I will, I don't mind."

Emily took the summer off from piano lessons. At her first lesson when we resumed in the fall she played through a piece and I asked, "Now didn't that feel nice and refreshing after not playing for so long?" She quickly responded with a firm "NO." When I asked, "How DID it feel?" she said "Annoying."

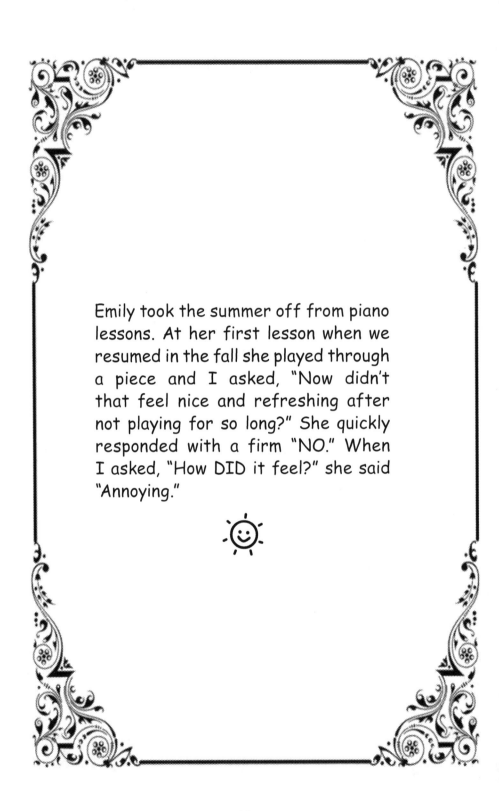

As Emily looked at the new piece I placed on the piano for her to play she said, "I hate you." Playing along I responded, "You hurt my feelings." Her comeback, "Don't worry about it, I hate everybody."

After Erin finished her lesson I called for her younger sister, "Emily its time for your piano lesson." She yelled from another room, "Let Dad take the lesson, he's the one that ordered the piano."

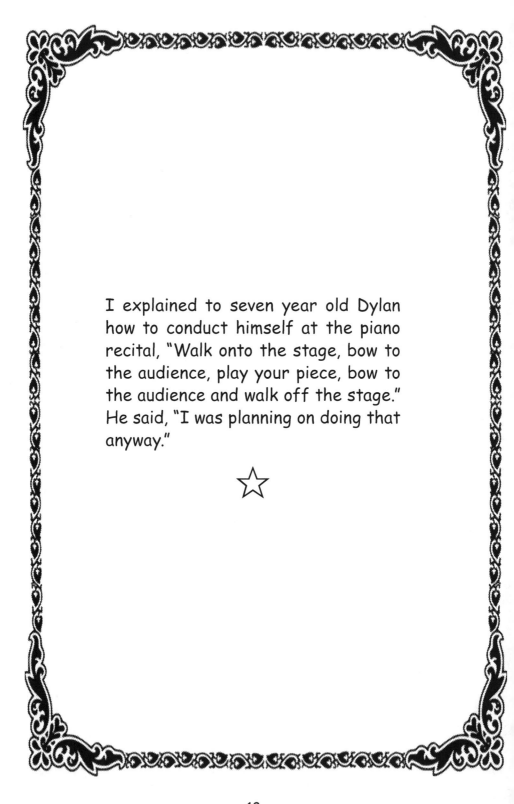

I explained to seven year old Dylan how to conduct himself at the piano recital, "Walk onto the stage, bow to the audience, play your piece, bow to the audience and walk off the stage." He said, "I was planning on doing that anyway."

☆

Eight Year Olds

When I reviewed Emily's written theory work I praised her for getting every answer correct. Her enthusiastic response. "can my reward be you leaving?"

While checking out Myles' understanding of his theory lesson I asked, "What do we call the scale that uses all the notes moving in half steps? He answered, "Moving in half steps? The Chromnomatic Scale."

While playing one of her songs Kara sneezed. She stopped and started over only to be interrupted with another sneeze in the same exact spot in the song. As she cupped her hands over her nose she moaned "I think I'm allergic to that note."

When Breanna was introduced to her Classic Themes piano book she studied an illustration of Bach on the cover and said, "That book's not nice, its got a picture of a mean old piano teacher on the front."

Breanna was solving Note Words in her Note Speller book. After solving one that spelled "baggage" she asked, "What's that?" I said, "What do you take with you on a trip?" Her response, "luggage."

Dylan was upstairs when he overheard me tell his mother about the piano recital I had scheduled for my students. When he came downstairs I asked, "Dylan, did you hear the good news?" He said, "I don't know if THAT'S good news." I then asked him if his older brothers would go to the recital to support him. Dylan scoffed, "Support? You mean criticize."

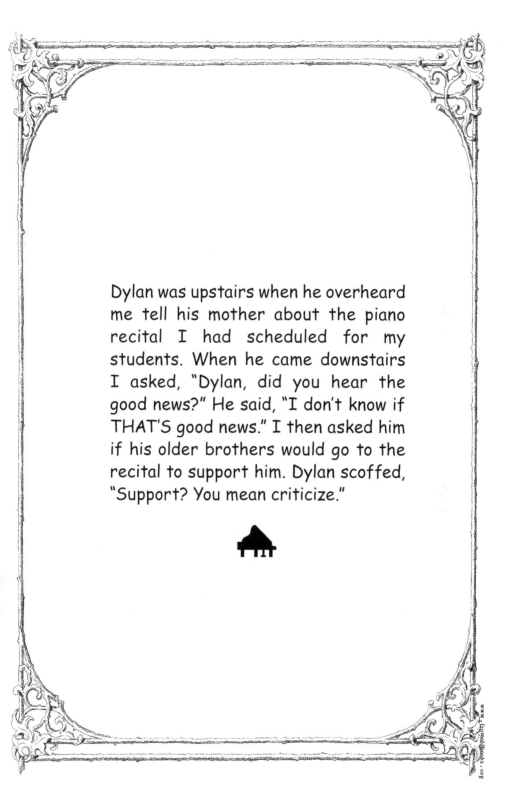

About ten minutes into Nick's lesson he asked if he could be finished. When I inquired why he replied, "My cereal is getting soggy."

After Mia played one of her songs she neglected to observe the repeat sign. When I brought it to her attention and asked her to repeat from the beginning she complained "you mean I just played all that for nothing?"

Alex displayed great technique on a piece she had learned but then struggled with sight reading a new piece. I said, "Your technique is developing well but your sight reading skills are suffering. We need to get your fingers and your brain on the same page." She responded, "But my mind and body aren't reading the same book."

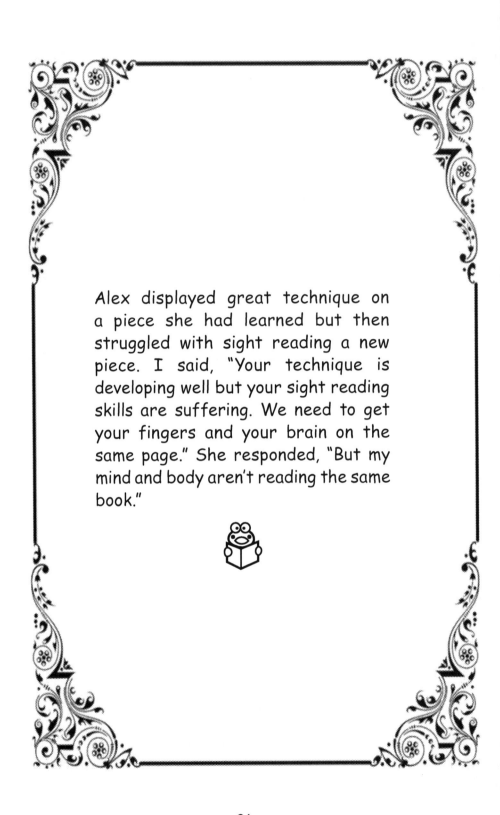

Nine Year Olds

Erika played her piece up to the "D C al fine" then stopped. I asked, "What does the D C mean?" Her reply, "Don't continue."

D.C.

I was giving Drake a pep-talk about practicing and commented that his parents would enjoy hearing him practice. Drake disagreed by pointing out "my mom doesn't like to hear irritating noises."

When I handed Shaina her new Alfred Level 1B books she got very excited and asked, "What happens when you finish all 6 levels?" I told her she would then be good enough to play Carnegie Hall. Shaina thought for a moment and then said, "Well you'll have to play it for me because I've never heard it."

Sean is a student that often gets frustrated. After sight-reading an easy piece perfectly I asked him why there would be an easy one in the book after several hard ones. He said, "To calm me down?"

When Chaz got to the bottom of the page of the piece he was playing I said, "There is a D C al fine. What does that mean?" His reply, "This song was made in Washington D. C?"

D.C.

After Mia confessed that she hadn't been practicing she asked if I was going to assign another piece. In a tone of disappointment I said, "Why should I? You probably won't practice that one either." Mia agreed with me commenting, "Yeah, but then I won't have to worry about not practicing."

Another piano student that had taken previous piano lessons was Eva. When reviewing with her she was unable to identify a time signature. I hinted with the question "when someone asks you to sign your name on important papers they ask for your...." Expecting her to say "signature" she replied "Hancock"

c

Sophia struggled to get through one of her pieces and forgot to repeat. I then quietly pointed to the repeat sign and she said, "I don't know THAT note."

Drake expressed an interest in playing blues piano so we had a lesson on the twelve bar blues form. As I explained that blues musicians repeat the twelve bars over and over he exclaimed "doesn't anyone notice?"

At Drake's first lesson I was reviewing what he had learned from his previous piano teacher. When I pointed to the treble clef and asked him what the music symbol was called he wasn't sure. I gave him a clue by asking "when you do something bad in school you may be in...." Expecting him to say "trouble", then think "treble", Drake asked "the principle's office?"

Continuing Drake's review I asked him to identify a quarter note. When he couldn't I hinted by asking him " what do you drop in a gumball machine?" Perplexed he said "50 cents?".

Cecile also plays violin and proudly informed me that she was being placed in Advanced Orchestra. Congratulating her progress I asked her what comes after Advanced Orchestra. She wondered "Over Advanced Orchestra?"

Alexandria and I shared with each other the sentences we use to remember the lines for both treble and bass clef. She mentioned hers as being "Elvis Goes Boogieing Down Fremont" and "Great Big Dreams For America" When I shared mine as being "Ernie Gave Bert Dirty French fries" and "Great Big Dogs Fight Animals." She snapped "You're so negative."

I asked Alex, "Why do they want us to play the first line loud and second line soft?" She replied, "They don't, they want ME to play the first line loud and the second line soft."

$$mf \quad mp$$

I had just assigned The Gift to be Simple as a new piece for David to play. He looked it over and said, "It should be called The Gift to be Complicated."

Lily had been taking lessons on a digital, electric piano and commented about her friend having a "real" piano. I asked if it was a "grand piano" and she enthusiastically responded "yes, but they chopped off the back and pushed it up against the wall."

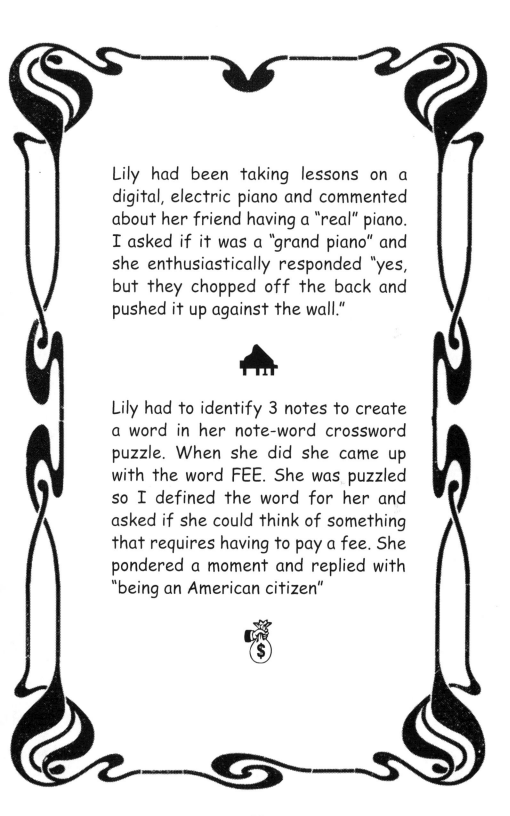

Lily had to identify 3 notes to create a word in her note-word crossword puzzle. When she did she came up with the word FEE. She was puzzled so I defined the word for her and asked if she could think of something that requires having to pay a fee. She pondered a moment and replied with "being an American citizen"

When Lily and I were having a discussion about time signatures I mentioned that there were others besides 4/4 and 3/4.
She slowly turned and looked at me and whispered "that sounds scary."

Shivering, I made a comment about how cold it was in Emily's house and she politely volunteered to start a fire in the fireplace. "But I don't see that you have any wood" I remarked. She said, "The piano's made of wood."

While Shaina was notating an F sharp in her theory book she asked, "what side of the note do you place the sharp sign?" I answered, "Since we read left to right the sign goes on the left so we see it first. We then know to sharp the note it's in front of." She inquired, "What if you're Jewish and can only read Hebrew?

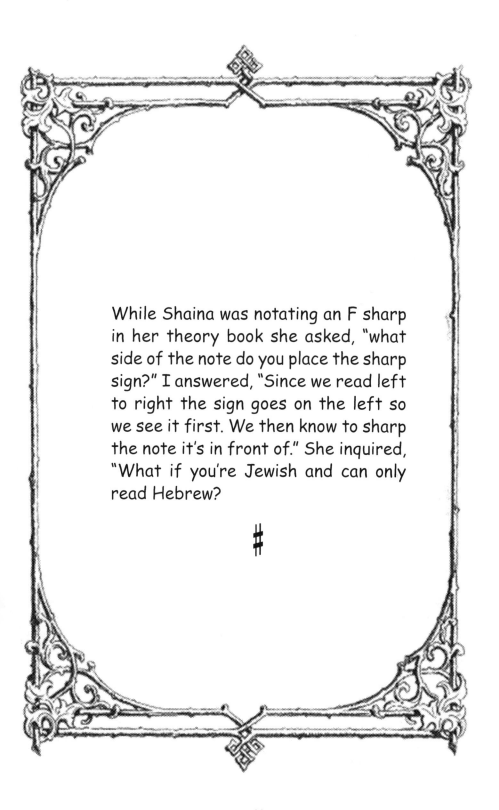

Ten Year Olds

I asked David what costume he wore for Halloween and his sarcastic response was, "I went as Darth Vader. What did you go as, a Piano Teacher?"

When Jessica played her new piece perfectly I said, "You're becoming a good sight reader. Do you know what sight reading is?" Jessica guessed, "When you don't look at your hands?"

Emily was sight reading the piece "That's a Fourth" which contains melodic 4ths. After playing the first line which was for only the right hand I said, "Good, now try the second line, which was for only the left hand." She said with concern, "I can't, my left hand has fourth-a-phobia."

♪

While introducing Katherine to the primary chords I playfully asked, "Hey, what's up with those Roman Numerals, they must mean something. Where do you suppose they come from?" Her sarcastic reply, "Rome...duh."

As I handed Katherine her Ear Training book to do melodic dictation I said, "Listen carefully, these can be tricky." Her immediate response, "These aren't tricky, they're evil."

As Savannah's lesson started she saw that her brother and her friend were cleaning her grandmother's silver. She was very upset she could not join them because cleaning the silver was one of her favorite things to do. As her lesson ended I asked, "Guess what?" Expecting her to happily reply, "My lesson is over?" she angrily said instead, "They're done cleaning the silver."

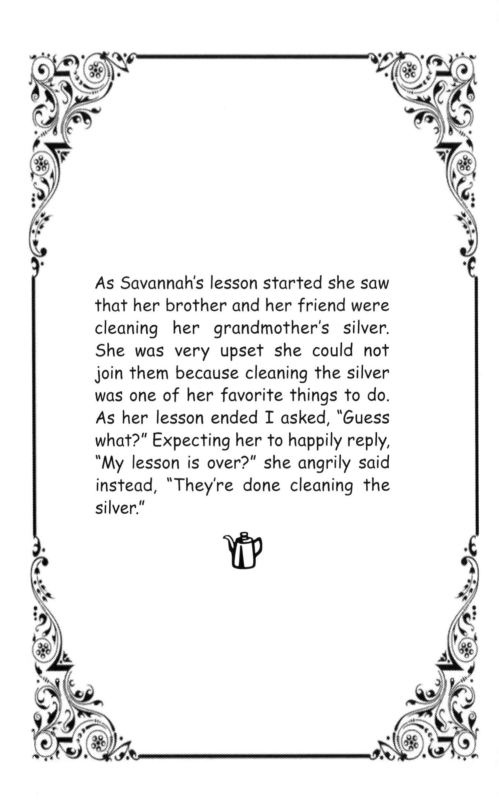

Eleven Year Olds

As she began her piano lesson Emily looked at her assigned lesson and breathed a big sigh. I said, "Oh Emily, its not that bad, its not like you're at the dentist." Emily pointedly said, "I don't mind the dentist."

David was complaining about having to practice his Hanon exercises. I told him that practicing will make his hands so strong that he'll be able to lift his piano over his head. He grumbled, "I can already do that."

Savannah forgot to flat the note "b" while playing a piece in F so I drew a courtesy flat sign in front of the note. She said, "That's what I played." I asked, "What did I just draw?" Savannah replied "a b". After taking a second look she yelled, "Oh, a flat sign."

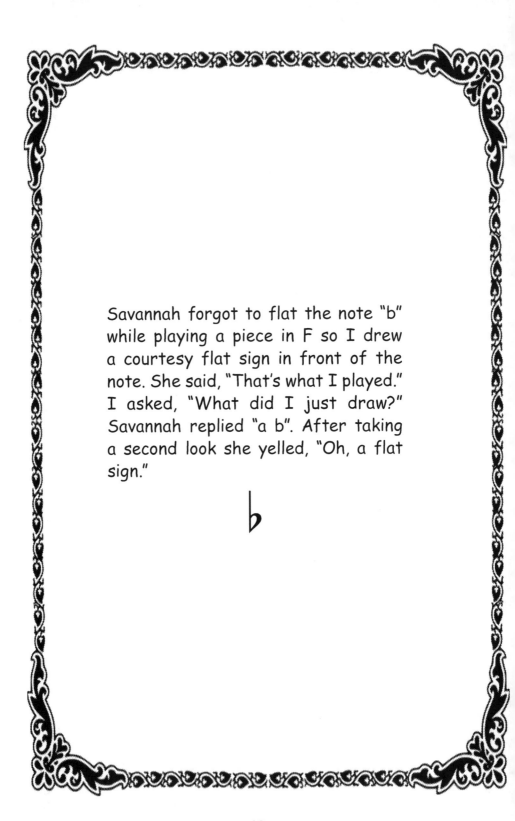

Cale always liked playing his pieces while making comical movements with his hands. I suggested he watch a Marx Brothers movie to see how Chico Marx played like that. Since Cale was too young to be familiar with the Marx Brothers he asked who they were. I explained they were brothers who made old black and white comedy movies and were very funny. Cale asked, "Black and white, were they adopted?"

Twelve Year Olds

As Christen was playing her piece during her lesson I accidentally let a yawn slip out. She noticed it and said, "I'm not THAT bad."

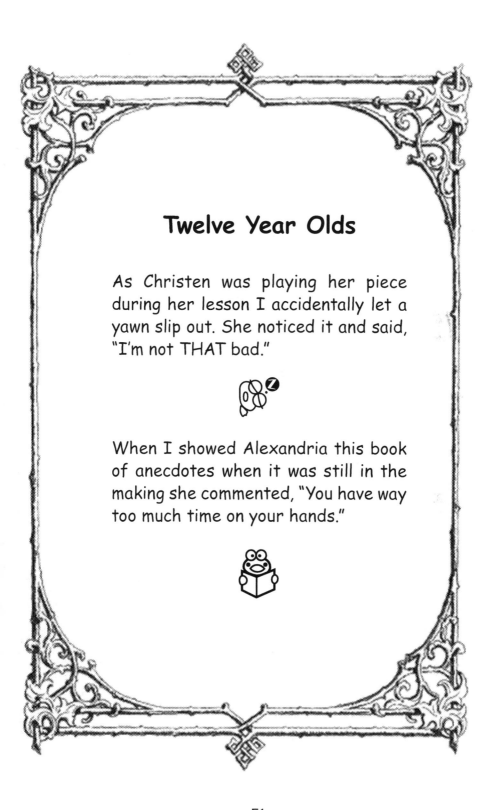

When I showed Alexandria this book of anecdotes when it was still in the making she commented, "You have way too much time on your hands."

When Jeremy asked why there was a sharp sign on a note that was already made sharp by the key signature I explained that it was called a courtesy sharp. As we moved on to theory he was assigned to draw a note on a ledger line above the staff. Upon completion he continued with adding another ledger line above the note he made. When I told him that the extra ledger line wasn't necessary he sarcastically explained "that's a courtesy ledger line."

Jeremy started playing a G position piece in C position so I stopped him and said, "Even though everything you just played sounded right it was actually wrong. Do you know why?" he responded, "Because you're here?"

When Nikki and I were discussing key signatures I asked her if she remembered what an accidental was. She curiously questioned back "when you accidentally play a sharp or flat in a song and you weren't suppose to?"

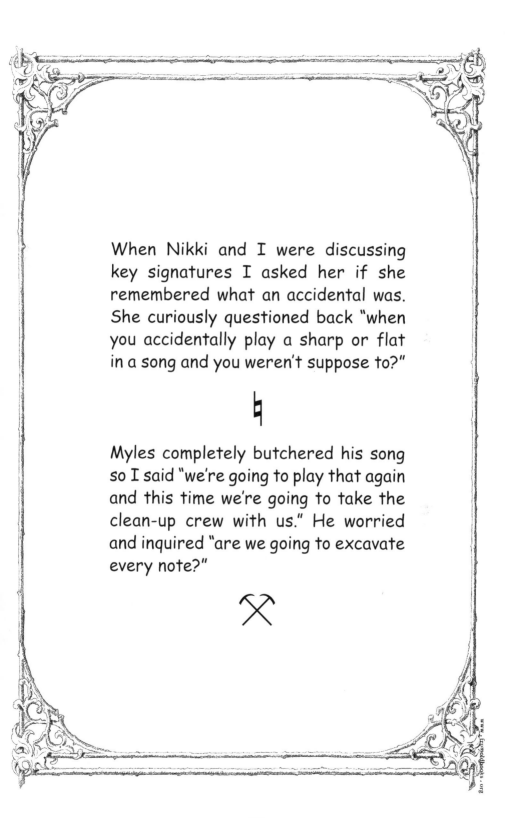

Myles completely butchered his song so I said "we're going to play that again and this time we're going to take the clean-up crew with us." He worried and inquired "are we going to excavate every note?"

Thirteen - Fifteen Year Olds

As Joseph was playing his scales I pointed out that he played one incorrectly. He firmly disagreed so I reminded him that I had been playing that particular scale for forty years. Joseph sarcastically asked "you mean you've been playing that scale wrong for forty years?"

The question asked to Alexandria was " what are the three types of minor scales?" She answered "harmonic, melodic and plutonic." I couldn't resist but to playfully comment "oh yes, the plutonic minor scale which of course is used extensively in HARD ROCK music."

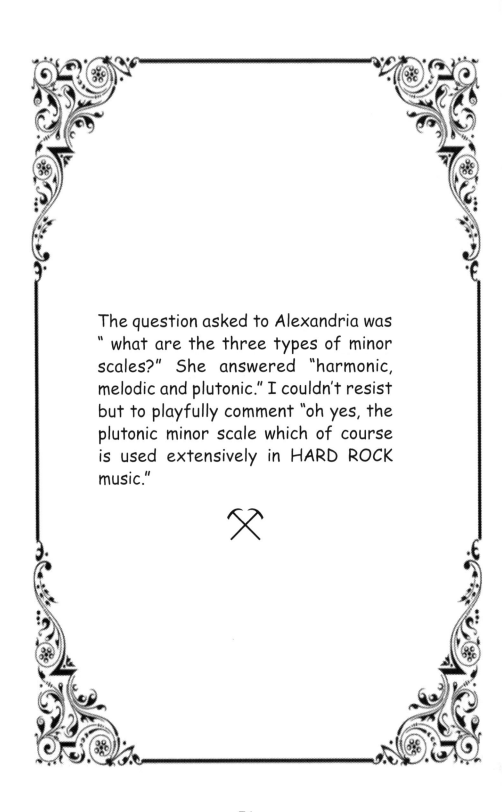

Cale played the last chord in his piece fortissimo with a fermata. As he held it out I reminded him, "That last chord was supposed to be played pianissimo." Cale said, "It'll get there."

During Doug's lesson the sound of his nine year old sister practicing the violin was coming from a nearby room. As she scratched through Twinkle, Twinkle Little Star her brother sighed and said, "I hope she gets better fast."

As fifteen year old Alexandra stumbled through the first two measures of Pizzicati by Delibes she stopped, looked at me and said, "Just kidding."

♪

During a lesson on improvisation Joseph noticed that I played a familiar melody while I was soloing. I explained that using something familiar while improvising is called "quoting". Joseph shot back "Oh really, I thought it was called plagiarism."

∞

When I assigned fifteen year old Lauren an ambitious piece of music she commented on how much practice it would take to learn it. Knowing her mother played the piano I jokingly said, "Mom will probably learn the piece before you do." Lauren's response, "I wouldn't doubt it, she has more time than I do."

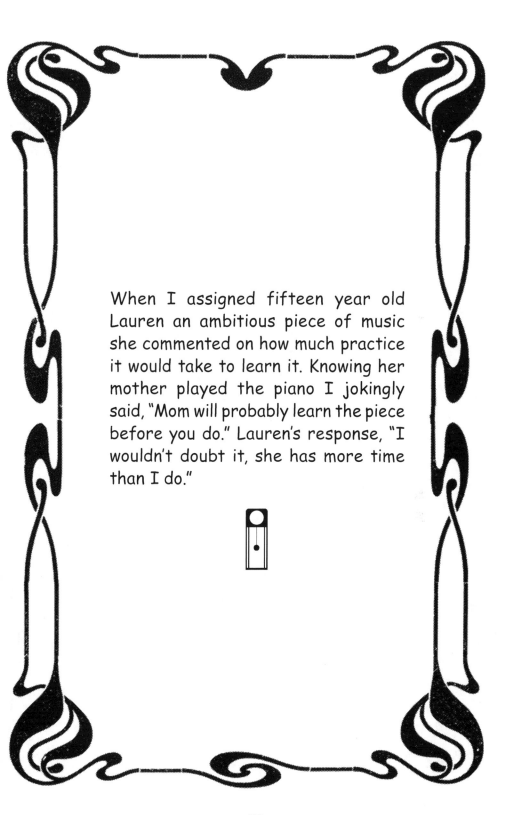

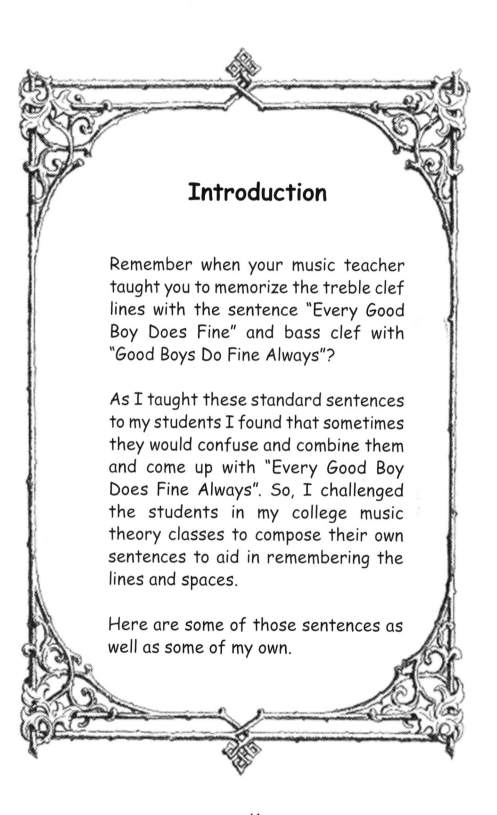

Introduction

Remember when your music teacher taught you to memorize the treble clef lines with the sentence "Every Good Boy Does Fine" and bass clef with "Good Boys Do Fine Always"?

As I taught these standard sentences to my students I found that sometimes they would confuse and combine them and come up with "Every Good Boy Does Fine Always". So, I challenged the students in my college music theory classes to compose their own sentences to aid in remembering the lines and spaces.

Here are some of those sentences as well as some of my own.

Treble Clef Lines - E G B D F

Every Good Band Deserves Fans

Ed Got Busted Driving fast

Ernie Gave Bert Dirty Frenchfries

Everyone Goes Bonkers During Football

Empty Garbage Before Dad Flips

Treble Clef Lines - E G B D F

Even Great Beethoven Drank Frequently

Electric Guitars Bear Distorted Feedback

Entice Girls By Driving Ferraries

Even Great Bassoonists Deserve Friends

Everyone Gets Bored Doing Finances

Treble Clef Lines - E G B D F

Epicureans Get Bloated Devouring Food

Every Good Burger Deserves Fries

Eddie Gomez, Bassist, Deserves Fame

Electricity Gave Birth Delivering Frankenstein

Exercise Gives Bodies Desired Fitness

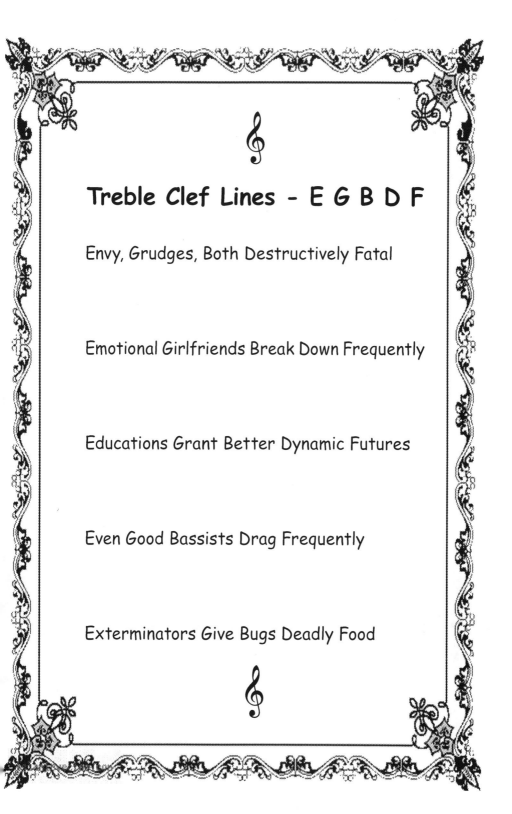

Treble Clef Lines - E G B D F

Envy, Grudges, Both Destructively Fatal

Emotional Girlfriends Break Down Frequently

Educations Grant Better Dynamic Futures

Even Good Bassists Drag Frequently

Exterminators Give Bugs Deadly Food

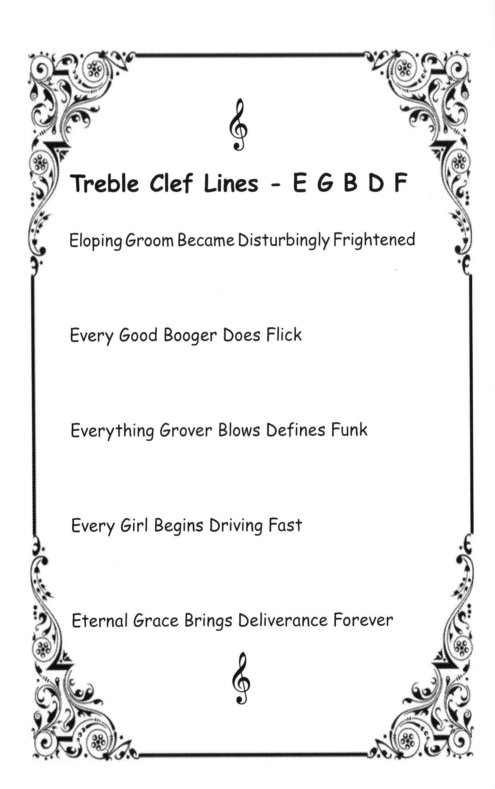

Treble Clef Lines - E G B D F

Eloping Groom Became Disturbingly Frightened

Every Good Booger Does Flick

Everything Grover Blows Defines Funk

Every Girl Begins Driving Fast

Eternal Grace Brings Deliverance Forever

Treble Clef Spaces - F A C E

Freedom Always Costs Everything

Flies Are Crap Eaters

Flutes And Clarinets Entertain

Fallen Angels Create Evil

Failed Another College Exam

Treble Clef Spaces - F A C E

Flipper Always Catches Eels

Fender Amps Cause Earaches

Forgive And Commend Enemies

Flaming Accordians Create Excitement

Fred Astaire Choreographed Everything

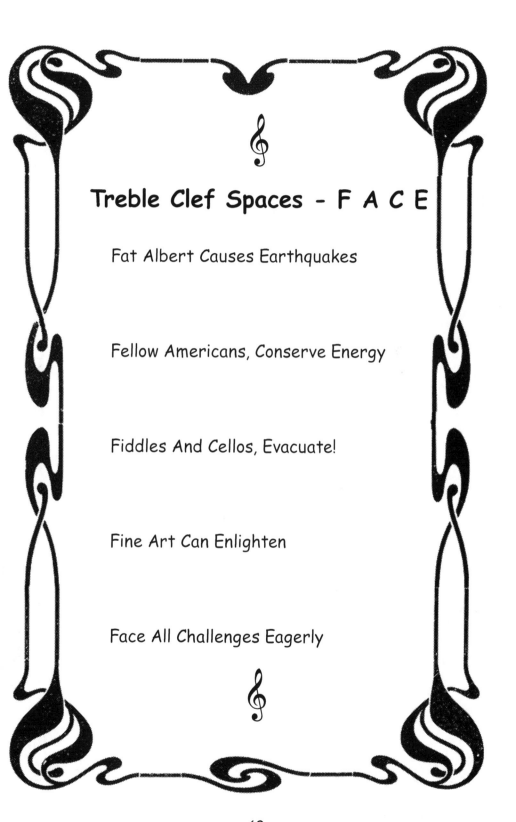

Treble Clef Spaces - F A C E

Fat Albert Causes Earthquakes

Fellow Americans, Conserve Energy

Fiddles And Cellos, Evacuate!

Fine Art Can Enlighten

Face All Challenges Eagerly

Treble Clef Spaces - F A C E

Fight And Conquer Evil

Ferociously Accomplish Chopin Etudes

Frequently Attend Concert Events

Fraternities Avoid College Educations

Fathers Are Children's Encouragers

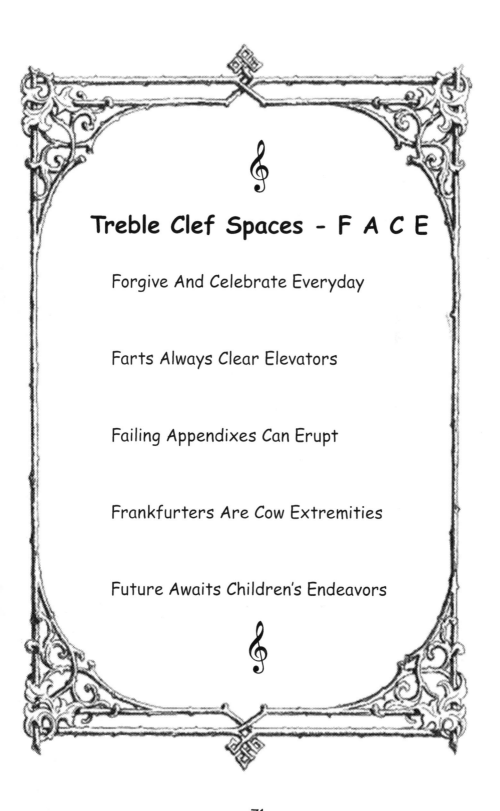

Treble Clef Spaces - F A C E

Forgive And Celebrate Everyday

Farts Always Clear Elevators

Failing Appendixes Can Erupt

Frankfurters Are Cow Extremities

Future Awaits Children's Endeavors

𝄢

Bass Clef Lines - G B D F A

Galleries Beautifully Display Fine Art

Good Bands Don't Fade Away

Go Beg Dad For Allowance

Garfield Bites Dogs For Amusement

Go Beyond Doors For Answers

𝄢

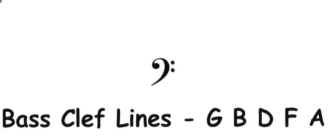

Bass Clef Lines - G B D F A

Guitar Broke During Final Audition

Girls Buy Diamonds For Accessories

George Bush Didn't Fix Anything

Give Blood Donations For All

Great Big Dreams For America

Bass Clef Lines - G B D F A

Going Bald Drives Females Away

Grasp Bob Dylan's Folk Attitude

Great Bellson's Drumming Fascinates Admirers

Gravity Brings Down Faulty Airplanes

Green Bay Defeats Falcons Always

𝄢 Bass Clef Lines - G B D F A

Good Bye Darling, Farewell, Adieu

Gallant Behavior Deserves Female Attention

Gimmicks Brilliantly Disguise False Advertising

Greedy Banks Discouraged Foreclosing Americans

Gorgeous Blonde Daughter Flourishes Ambition

𝄢

𝄢

Bass Clef Lines - G B D F A

God's Beauty Derives From All

Gross Bathrooms Discharge Foul Aromas

Good Boys Don't Forget Anniversaries

Good Boys Deserve Full Allowances

George Benson Does Funky Arrangements

𝄢

Bass Clef Spaces - A C E G

Aeolian Chords Evoke Grief

Amps Can Electrocute Guitarists

All Composers Envy Gershwin

Attack Cinderella's Enchanted Garden

Alice Cooper Enjoys Golf

Bass Clef Spaces - A C E G

Armstrong's Cornet Entertains God

All Cowboys Emit Gas

Amazing Clapton Enjoys Guitar

At Christmas Exchange Gifts

All Conductors Expect Glory

Bass Clef Spaces - A C E G

Another Claim, Eureka! Gold!

Aaron Copland Euphony Gratifies

Avocados Create Excellent Guacamole

Always Compliment Every Girl

All Chefs Enjoy Gastronomy

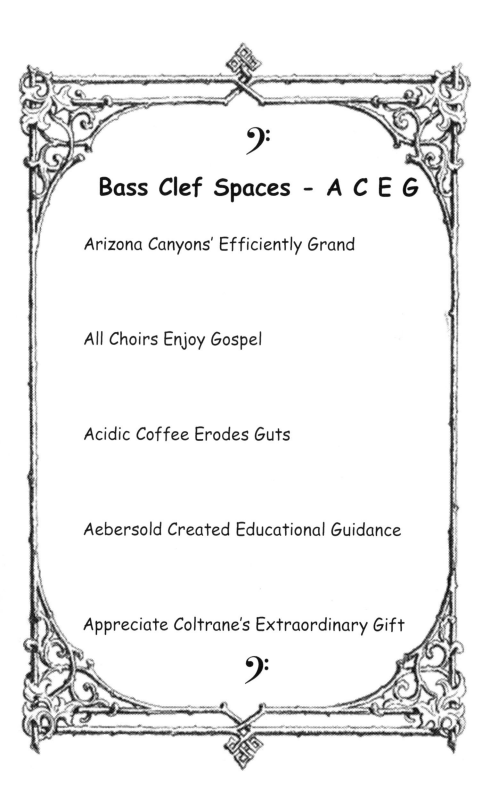

Bass Clef Spaces - A C E G

Arizona Canyons' Efficiently Grand

All Choirs Enjoy Gospel

Acidic Coffee Erodes Guts

Aebersold Created Educational Guidance

Appreciate Coltrane's Extraordinary Gift

Bass Clef Spaces - A C E G

Acquire Countless Electric Guitars

Advocate Charitable Environmental Groups

Always Catch Ellington Gigs

All Creative Energy Grows

Always Carry Eternal Grace

Printed in the United States
By Bookmasters